Y0-BZY-453

FROM A HEALING HEART

BY

SUSAN WHITE-BOWDEN

Susan White-Bowden

Marjorie White

WHITE-BOWDEN ASSOCIATES

2863 Benson Road
Finksburg, Maryland 21048
(410) 833-3280

Text by Susan White-Bowden
Photography by Marjorie White and Susan White-Bowden
Dust Jacket by Gateway Press, Baltimore, Maryland

Library of Congress Catalog Card Number 87-80962
ISBN 0-9633762-1-7

First printing, 1987
Revised Second Printing, 1993

Printed by Dai Nippon Printing Company, Ltd.
Tokyo, Japan

TO THE MEMORY OF JODY

In the shadow of his life is love
In the shadow of his death is pain
In spite of the hurt I'm so glad he lived

CHAPTERS OF SURVIVAL

1. ACCEPTANCE

2. FORGIVENESS AND FAITH

3. LIVE JUST TO LIVE

4. THE NURTURING OF NATURE

5. COMMUNICATION

6. LAUGHTER

7. SHARING

8. FACING THE FUTURE

9. SPECIAL DAYS

10. COMFORT IN CARING

11. GOING ON WITH HOPE

MARJORIE WHITE

6

INTRODUCTION

In 1974 my former husband committed suicide. In 1977, two and a half years later, my beloved seventeen-year-old son, Jody, also committed suicide. People have asked me how I survived not just one, but two such tragedies, and am still able to find pleasure and joy in my life.

I've asked myself that same question, and I've searched for the answers that might help others trying to live through any loss.

I believe that the death of a child is the greatest loss a person can endure. But living through divorce or the death of a mother or father, a husband or wife, or a friend, leaves a wound that must be allowed to heal. The pain will be there and must not be repressed. You must grieve; until you grieve the healing won't start.

However it is so easy to say, "Why me?" It's hard not to feel sorry for ourselves and to allow anger, and even hate, to creep in and take over our feelings.

The anger may be directed at those who left us, at life itself or at God, for allowing such tragedies. Perhaps most destructive of all is the anger and hatred directed at ourselves, believing that if we were good people this wouldn't have happened to us.

But there is too much in life to love to let bitterness take over the beauty around us. And we should not let the pain of our lost loves take over our lives blocking out the others we love and who love us. These are people who can help make us feel alive and vital again, people who depend on us for the same kind of feelings.

Even if we are left all alone, nature surrounds us with the promise of comfort and change and a better tomorrow.

We know so painfully well the person who has left us. But we don't know about the lives in our future. If we don't give those unknown lives, and our own life, a chance to be known, we give up on the possibility of our future happiness. We give up on our future. Although the lives of those who have left us may be frozen in time, our lives are not. We must not allow the pain of the present to obscure the fullness of our future.

I hope by sharing my thoughts, words, and pictures that you might begin to understand that even behind the darkest of clouds *there is* sunshine and *it will*, eventually, be revealed to us.

I have met dozens of people who have suffered painful losses. They will carry the memory of that pain for the rest of their lives, as I will. But we have gone on to find the secret of strength in survival.

There is no precise formula for living through personal tragedy, but what follows are, at least, some of the necessary ingredients for making it beyond that agonizing time when you think all is lost and life just isn't worth the struggle to go on. I believe it is. I know it is.

I speak not as a doctor, psychologist or teacher. I am none of those.

I speak as a person whose heart was so deeply wounded that I was absolutely certain I would die. I did not. And so I speak . . . from a healing heart.

9

Seeds of Hope

Amidst the weeds of worry,
even in a field of pain,
grow little seeds of hope,
bright spots to look for,
to savor and cling to.
The flowers of our future.
The promises that the pain will end,
making room for the blossoms of joy.

CHAPTER 1

ACCEPTANCE

Denial Delays The Healing Process

Whether it's a broken relationship or a death, to deny that it's final makes it impossible to go on.

We must accept what has happened and live through the grief of loss. We must begin to look beyond, and stop looking back.

To try to recapture or re-create what was is to avoid and perhaps abort what might be.

The bittersweet memories of what was, and what might have been, will always be within easy recall, but dwelling upon the past will hinder the healing that is the path to future happiness.

MARJORIE WHITE

In the weeks that followed Jody's suicide, every day seemed like a lifetime.

Each sunrise brought a painful beginning, like birth. However, unlike birth, where there is eventually joy, there was a daily struggle to face the reality of a deep, irreplaceable loss. It was like going through labor, but there was no new life to compensate for the pain; there was only more pain because my baby was dead. The loss of a newborn is painful enough, but my son had given me seventeen years of precious memories before he aborted himself. At night, the darkness, like death from old age, would bring a quiet, resigned surrender to my child's end, and hopefully my own. In the morning of the next day, dismayed by my own survival, the pain would be fresh and another twenty-four hour life cycle would begin. In between morning and night I somehow existed, and eventually was able to pretend everything was okay, trying very hard to go on with my life in a positive, productive way. Those around me even saw the smiles of someone they assumed was adjusting amazingly well.

In private, I was fighting the finality of my son's death, not wanting to believe or accept that I would never see him again. At times I raged and wailed that such a thing could happen.

I have known others who have experienced the death of someone very close and dear to them to just stop functioning for a period of time. They stopped performing even the simplest of tasks, such as making coffee. They just stopped doing almost everything except praying that death would also devour them. What they sought was an end to their tortured existence, an easy way out. But there is no easy way out of this life, and each leaving sets off a chain reaction of pain for those left behind.

I began to focus on the others around me, feeling I must do so for the sake of my two daughters, but I too desired death. I thought, at the time, how easy suicide would be. How easy it would have been, right after Jody's death, to follow in his footsteps. Thank God I was thinking about others at that time and not myself, and what I thought I wanted.

My life would have ended, causing the same kind of pain for those who love me, and I would never have known the incredible joy that lay ahead. Never would I have seen my daughters married or known the love of my grandchildren. I would have died without knowing the fulfillment of a good marriage. I would have destroyed all that was in my future. However, it's hard to care about a future when the present is so laden with pain.

At the end of August, several months after my son's death, I sought relief and change by going to Ocean City, Maryland, the resort where we had spent a family vacation the summer before.

I went alone so I could think, and remember, and cry as I wished, without prying questions or intruding looks from well-meaning loved ones who felt they needed to guard me, or monitor my mental stability.

I walked the beach wishing for that which could not be, could never be again. I sat in the sand, in front of the beach house where we had stayed, and relived, with the agony of grief as my guide, the moments we'd spent there. In fact, I went over our whole life together. The time we'd had together was too short, and I didn't know, when it was passing, how precious. No one warned me that my time with my son might not last or endure. I never dreamed that I would only have seventeen years with him, or that the past summer would be the last one. We'd all been happy that last summer at the beach. I guess I thought I could recapture some of those feelings in my search for some relief from the pain that I could hardly stand, caused by a loss that I didn't want to accept as forever.

I kept hoping Jody would walk out of the beach house to go for a swim with me. He didn't, and I knew he wouldn't. I began to dwell on where he was. I pictured my precious child beneath that mound of dirt back on our farm.

I wanted to dig it away, to uncover my Jody and hold his body in my arms. "Oh dear God," I thought, "I'm going crazy." I couldn't help it, I just wanted him back. I pictured his smooth young face beneath the dark blonde hair, his hazel eyes and warm smile that always brightened his entire expression—and mine. I could almost feel his strong body and powerful arms. I closed my eyes and made myself listen as I recalled his voice. "Aw, mom, you don't really want me to do that. If I clean up the back porch you'll have nothing to bug me about." It was the gravelly voice of a teenage boy entering manhood. It was the voice of my son. I didn't ever want to forget the sound of that voice. I would consciously keep bringing it back over and over again so I wouldn't forget it, so I wouldn't lose Jody in the only form I had left, my memory.

It was the first of September when I got home from the beach.

First I unloaded the car. That's like me to do what I think I should before I do what I want.

Then, almost hesitantly at first, I began the walk to the

newly established graveyard in the hillside pasture. The tall pasture grass, left unmown that summer, parted with passive acceptance as I made my way toward my son's burial ground.

From about one hundred feet away something caught my eye. Something that produced tears and caused my heart to speed up, as did my feet.

I ran the rest of the way and fell to my knees beside the *almost* bare mound of dirt.

As a little boy Jody loved to pick Black-eyed Susans. He'd pick those wild flowers and bring them to me with such love and pride in presentation.

The last bunch he picked for me was on my birthday before his death, August 4, 1976.

The Black-eyed Susan is an independent wild flower that can not be forced to grow out of season. Even the blanket of Black-eyed Susans placed on the winner of the prestigious preakness horse race are really painted daisies. That race is run in May before the Black-eyed Susans cover the Maryland countryside, and they can't be forced to grow in greenhouses. Black-eyed Susans grow from seeds, and do not return from the same roots year after year. The growing period for these wild flowers is the middle of June to the middle of August.

But there, the first of September in the year of my son's death, in the center of Jody's grave, was a single perfectly formed Black-eyed Susan. It stood with strength and reassurance. It was all alone in the still, unsettled dirt covering the grave. There was not even a blade of grass or a single weed around.

JOHN O'DONNELL WHITE, JR.
(JODY)
MARCH 8, 1960 — MAY 9, 1977
HIS LIFE BROUGHT US GREAT JOY
HIS DEATH GREAT PAIN
OUR LOVE FOR HIM IS ETERNAL

I wept with mixed emotions of intense loss and love, feeling both distance and closeness, sadness and sudden relief.

I saw it as a sign from my darling Jody. It spoke to me words from my dead child. "Do not cry. Do not despair. I love you and never intended for you to suffer so much. Please forgive me, and please be happy with the rest of your life. Please believe that I'm okay, and at peace."

Whether it was a sign from Jody or from God; perhaps a bird dropped a Black-eyed Susan seed on the fresh grave, it brought me relief. I felt that my son wasn't so far away, and that his spirit would always be with me.

If nothing more, it helped me to begin to think of Jody there, at the gravesite. He was dead, and I began to accept that. I started to realize that I would never again see his form as I had known it. But his spirit would be close and would guide me. I would not forget him and what we shared. He would always be special. What we gave to one another, what we had meant to each other, would not die or diminish with the passage of years, and it has not. Each year since Jody's death, a single Black-eyed Susan has grown on his grave.

It is a comfort and a joy. It is a remarkable phenomenon that now makes me smile rather than cry.

Jody was a kid who never forgot my birthday, and never outgrew giving his mom flowers. I choose to believe he still hasn't.

There are many mysteries in life and death that can't be explained, and I think shouldn't be, just accepted.

A new love: my granddaughter Emily, born March of 1983.

New Loves

Lost loves can never be
forgotten or replaced.
But if we allow it
the heart grows bigger
to make room for new loves.

"If I couldn't forgive John and Jody, I couldn't forgive myself"

CHAPTER 2

FORGIVENESS AND FAITH

Forgiveness may be the most valuable key to surviving a loss without the ugly scar tissue of bitterness and blame.

Have you ever noticed how much easier it is to hate than to love when life deals us an unfair blow?

Especially in divorce, or a tragic death, we are quick to point the unforgiving finger of blame. Someone must be at fault, therefore someone must be punished. Often it is ourselves we blame and then hate.

Even when we direct our anger at those around us, we are the ones who suffer the most.

We cannot heal while we are hating.

Jody and his father are now buried side by side in our family cemetery. That wasn't the case at first.

The graveyard was established with Jody's death. I had insisted that my son be buried on our property so he would be nearby. John's remains had been placed elsewhere.

It was my daughters who wanted them together, Marjorie in particular. Marjorie is the oldest child, and was the closest to her dad. We argued when she pleaded with me to move her father's "cremains." There were bitter words and tears. At the time, I was hating my former husband for the example he had set for Jody by killing himself. I didn't want him in any way to be a part of what I now shared with my son. I didn't want him around when I went to be by Jody's side.

I hated John and what he had done. I resented the fact that he had ever lived, and hated myself for once loving him and allowing him to be the father of my children.

I had been building the bitter case against John from the moment of our son's suicide. But I didn't allow myself to feel anger toward Jody for leaving me. He was my baby, and in my eyes he could do no wrong. I felt he was too young to be held accountable for his actions, which I now realize was not true. But I didn't see that then.

My daughters finally convinced me that it would be comforting for them to have their father and brother buried together, and so I agreed. It was an important move, because it began the forgiving process in me, and thus allowed the healing to begin.

If I couldn't forgive John for the part he played in Jody's suicide, I could never forgive myself for what I felt was my role in both suicides. The truth is that I felt tremendously responsible for both. Forgiving John helped me to find the compassion to forgive myself, and allowed me to forgive Jody for the pain he left me with by killing himself.

The most remarkable example of forgiveness I've ever heard about comes from the most loving woman I've ever met. Mary Carter Smith is a writer and folklorist. She calls herself a "griot" after the story tellers of Africa. In 1978, her only child was murdered. Ricardo "Ricky" Carter was twenty-nine at the time. He was an artist; gentle, sensitive, and a joy to all who knew him. There were no words to describe the pleasure Ricky brought to his mother. There were no words to describe the devastation she felt when the phone rang and she was told her beloved child had been stabbed to death by a woman he barely knew, a woman he had brushed against in a bar. She later said that he touched her behind. Because of that she pulled out a twelve-inch knife and slashed his throat. The anger and pain Mary felt were indescribable when she went to the medical examiner's office and watched as a dirty white blanket with red roses on it was pulled back to reveal the deadly still body of her warm and loving son. She says that she discovered the meaning of temporary insanity. She screamed and went wild. She says that if the woman who had killed her child had been within her reach, her hands would have easily found their way to that woman's neck. She truly believes that at that moment she would have squeezed until the murderer also experienced death.

And yet within twenty-four hours, Mary Carter Smith began forgiving what many would call unforgivable. And with her deep faith in God as her guide, she went to the woman's mother to console her.

Mary offered love and understanding and sympathy for that other mother's pain. She offered forgiveness for the daughter who took away her son.

Several years later at a prison work release program where Mary had been asked to speak and perform, she and her son's murderer came face to face. The woman, who had been arrogant and defiant in court, was now broken and remorseful. She begged for Mary's forgiveness.

"I've already forgiven you, child," Mary said as she took her into her understanding arms. Surprisingly, the revelation which occured at that moment came to Mary and not to the other woman.

It was then that Mary realized that this woman, who killed her only child, was now her "God" child. Mary felt a sense of responsibility directly from God. Here was a suffering soul in need of a humanitarian, someone with gentleness and wisdom who could guide and help her.

And that's what she did.

Mary helped her find a job and a new direction to her life. She helped her turn a wretched and meaningless existence into one that mattered.

Mary Carter Smith believes in a forgiving God, and she is a most forgiving woman.

One only needs to look into the peaceful eyes of this gentle woman to know the self-benefits of such love and forgiveness. Those dark eyes lead to the brightest, most bitter-free soul I've ever seen.

There is a goodness within this woman that has grown stronger in spite of, or perhaps because of, her pain.

She refused to let her suffering suffocate her belief in God and her fellow human beings.

She knows how easily we can want to hurt someone else when we are hurt. But more importantly, she's learned the blessings of loving instead.

She knows that to err is human, to forgive is divine.

With divine guidance and inner strength, she forgave, and her heart healed.

Faith

As Mary Carter Smith knows, having a deep belief in a supreme being, a loving and powerfully comforting God can help in your ability to accept, forgive, share and go on.

If you believe in the power of prayer, the consolation that can come from quiet conversations with your creator, you are likely to find comfort and direction.

I've asked for strength and it has been granted. I've asked for guidance and been shown the way. I often think I didn't ask soon enough, but when I did I was given the power to help myself and others.

"How in the world can I go on . . . ?"

CHAPTER 3

LIVE JUST TO LIVE

We clung together, sobbing and sharing each other's pain. Her's fresh and agonizing, mine years old but pulled to the surface by her devastating loss. Her son had also committed suicide.

"How in the world can I go on living?" she begged for answers. "Will I ever want to live again? Will I ever feel like smiling? How do you do it? How have you done it?"

My words sounded trite as I spoke them, but I knew they were good advice because it was what got me beyond the darkest hours of my life.

"Live today just to live. Eventually, sometime, somewhere, you will discover that you are once again living because you want to."

I told her that she might be meandering aimlessly through a department store and think, "I'd like to try on that dress," or maybe think, "we need a chair for the living room," and realize that she was thinking about tomorrow, that she was thinking beyond today, that she was once again caring about how she looked, or about her family's comfort.

One woman, whose husband had died, told me that she realized that she had begun to heal when she started to clean the house.

She had always kept their house neat and clean because her husband liked it that way. After his death she had let things go. She didn't have the energy to do housework, and she didn't really think about the mess she was living in. One day she noticed, and started cleaning because she wanted the house straight.

She was on the road to recovery.

The first woman, whose son committed suicide, also asked me about going back to work.

"How can I face the people I work with? How can I answer their questions?"

I told her that I found going back to work helpful in the healing process.

Oh, it's extremely difficult just to get up and get dressed when the pain of losing someone you love has left you physically and emotionally weak. It would be much easier to give up, and give in to the urge just to stay home, in bed.

It takes a great deal of strength and self-discipline to do it. But I've learned that self-discipline can be very beneficial in the ordeal of going on.

I told this woman, searching through her grief for answers, that when I went back to work I found my co-workers very supportive. Their questions, though few, helped me begin to open up. I was honest with my answers even though it was painful for me, and sometimes awkward for them.

A week later I saw the same woman. She took my hands in hers, and told me, with renewed strength and energy, that she had gone back to work.

She proudly shared with me this personal accomplishment, and as she did . . . she smiled.

David and Great Granddaddy
"They had some time together"

Reason to Live

*When you realize how fragile
each life is,
you understand how precious
each day is.*

Signs of Survival

Signs of survival are all around us,
in the shifting sands and the roaring seas,
ever changing, while remaining constant.
There is comfort in the clouds, in the birds,
in the sunrises and sunsets.

CHAPTER 4

THE NURTURING OF NATURE

Whenever I've felt the most alone, the most isolated from life, I've looked around and realized that we are never, ever entirely alone. Whenever I've wondered about the reasons for living, I've gotten answers from other forms of life surrounding us, which never questions why. Nature gives us only reasons to go on—never reasons to give in.

Sound of the Surf

The sounds of the surf
The salt of the sea
Healing medicine for you and me
Strong and certain and reassuring
Untiring tides— Unending waves
Soothing and comforting and company.
I'm never lonely when on the sand by the sea
Forever close to the memory of thee

Promise of Spring

The sounds of geese are over head
The spider has left it's intricate bed
The warmth of life seems so far away
The chill in the air seems certain to stay
But beyond the cold is the promise of spring
The birth and love and hope that it brings

Fire and Ice

Even in the dead of winter
The sun rises to warm the earth
To melt the icy daggers of despair
A burning glow of strength and survival

Secret of Survival

From nature comes a secret of survival.
While some will falter and fall from a perfect perch,
others will rebuild each nest destroyed.
While some give up without reason,
others achieve greatness in the face of doom.
Some will go on soaring though left alone,
gaining strength from the struggle of their flight.
Survivors seem to sense the sun behind the clouds,
weathering a storm just to glimpse a rainbow.
On the wings of life there are gentle currents and rough winds.
Survivors float and fight as each day dictates,
their hearts set determinedly on the horizon of hope.
The light they follow is their will to live.
The reward they receive is life itself.

MARJORIE WHITE

"So right were his words that I knew instantly that I was wrong"

CHAPTER 5

COMMUNICATION

Make a real effort to express your real feelings. Talk about them even if it's uncomfortable to do so.

Comfort will come with understanding.

Speak even when it's difficult. Search for the words that can free pent up emotions, can pull people together, and produce health and healing.

Words can help us all grow. They can help us express love, and they allow us to learn from one another.

We must not let the pain and suffering of loss silence our desire to share with words.

Words can make such a big difference. Let me explain how much they meant to me at one critical period of my life.

In the spring of 1979 happiness had begun to be a real part of my life again. I was starting to laugh more than I cried. I was healing, and daring to reach for the golden ring that could pull together two fragile and fragmented families.

I had decided to marry Jack Bowden, the man I had been dating when my son killed himself.

It was June 10th. At thirty-nine I was fulfilling my childhood dream of being a June bride.

The ceremony was held on the lawn of my house, on our family farm, a house that was about to become mine and Jack's. The same house where my son and his father had committed suicide. But no one allowed himself or herself to think about that on this joyous day.

A yellow and white striped tent sheltered about one hundred guests from a sudden shower as they waited for the wedding to begin.

Then moments later, as the clouds swiftly moved to the east, the tent diffused and filtered a strong afternoon sun. We were bathed in a radiant veil of gold. My father guided me gently but nervously across the lawn and down the aisle between the two sections of folding chairs.

My two grown daughters, Marjorie and O'Donnell, were my maids of honor. Jack's eight year old son, Christopher, was his best man. Our friend, the Reverend Fred Hanna, spoke the words, that we repeated, after which he pronounced us husband and wife.

There was a warmth of love and family that enveloped all who shared with us on that special day. Everyone was hoping, as I was, that tragedy was behind us and that only happiness lay ahead.

Two months later lightning struck our house, and it was gutted by fire. My mother called Jack at the television station, where he was anchoring the news, to tell him that our house was engulfed in flames.

I was downtown and knew nothing of what awaited me at home. I stopped at the grocery store to get dinner. I sang along with a familiar tune on the car radio as I happily anticipated another wonderful evening with my new and deeply loved husband.

When I crested the hill on Deer Park Road leading to our long country driveway, I was shocked to see fire engines lining the road. I pulled to the side of the road and stopped. My reporter instinct and training took over as I ran for details. My neighbor, Chuck Knight, was the first person I saw.

"What's going on? What happened?" I asked.

I'll never forget his expression.

He didn't know what to say, but quickly chose the honest direct approach. He tried to soften the blow by taking my hand in his.

"Don't you know?," he questioned, hoping I did.

"Know what?," I asked, my heart began to pound.

"It's your house. It was struck by lightning. We had a terrible storm out here. The worst in years."

My knees went weak. My heart seemed to burst with pain. My eyes, so used to crying, once again filled with burning tears that stung my face like alcohol on an open wound.

"I can't take anymore," I confessed to my neighbor. "When will it ever end? I just can't go through anymore." I pulled away from him and in a daze I began walking up the driveway. Jack was coming down the road towards me. I could see smoke lifting into the summer sky behind him. We stumbled into each other's arms.

"I can't take anymore, Jack," I sobbed with devastating certainty. "This is it. I just can't go on. I don't have enough strength left." Jack gently brushed the tears from my face and pulled me back into his arms, holding me very, very tight. I heard his words so soft and strong next to my ear. So right were those words that I knew instantly that I was wrong. I knew that I could go on. That we would not only endure this, but be better because of it.

He said, "Look, your things from your former life burned, and my things from my former life burned. Now we'll build ours."

And that's what we did. But it was Jack's words that got us started. They provided the solace and strength and encouragement which allowed us to clear away the charred ruins of what had been, making way for the new foundation of what could be.

"At that point I couldn't help but laugh through the tears"

CHAPTER 6

LAUGHTER

Laughter is the best medicine, and can lighten the heaviest burden of grief. However, most people are very uncomfortable when something humorous occurs during periods of mourning.

It is my feeling that when a smile replaces the frown of sadness, and tears of laughter momentarily take over for those of grief, we should welcome the change. It occurs so rarely during times of personal loss we should embrace those occurrences with unrestrained relief.

Laughter, after all, is a natural and normal release. The works of famous playwrights from Shakespeare to Neil Simon clearly show us the fine line between tragedy and comedy, and how easily that line can be crossed.

After our house fire in the summer of 1979, we had moved into an apartment, while our burned-out home was being rebuilt.

One day at work I got a call from a man who had been a dear friend of my first husband. He had moved to Texas, and we had lost touch with one another. It had been years since we had had any form of contact; at least six years. He knew nothing of what had happened in our lives, not even that John and I had divorced. He called to say that he was in town and would love to see us.

"How's John," he began.

"Hugh," I said, knowing where the conversation was going, but not knowing how to stop it, "John is dead."

"My God," he said. "What happened?"

"Suicide," I said. "He killed himself."

"Oh, how awful. You poor thing. What about the kids? How's Jody?"

"I don't know how to tell you this, but Jody's dead, too."

"Jesus Christ: How? When? What happened?"

"He also committed suicide, two and a half years after John did."

"I can't believe it," said our distraught friend, whom I'm sure was now wishing he had never picked up the phone to call me.

He asked with hesitation, "My God, Susan, how are you doing, and what about the girls? Can I come out to the house and see you?"

"I'm sorry, Hugh," I said as gently as I could, "but lightning struck our house last summer and fire completely gutted it. We're living in an apartment right now."

"I can't believe it. I can't believe any of it," he said, floundering for words of condolences and afraid to ask any more questions.

He said goodbye and hung up the phone. I haven't heard from him since.

When I put down the receiver, I couldn't help but laugh through the tears that were running down my face. It was like a comedy routine. The one that asks, "Is that what's bothering you bunky?" One tragedy on top of another until it becomes ridiculous. It sounded so absurd that it seemed unbelievable, which made it funny.

And so I laughed even as I cried, and it eased a very painful moment of reality for me.

I hope Hugh has since seen the comedy of that agonizing situation.

In the summer of 1986, my mother died. She was eighty-one and had, as they say, a long and good life. However, that didn't ease the grief for my eighty-two year old father. Her death ended a fifty-three year marriage that was a very special love story. For many of those years she served as a receptionist in his dental office. They spent twenty-four hours a day together, three hundred and sixty-five days a year. They worked together, vacationed together, raised their children and enjoyed their grandchildren and great-grandchildren together.

With her death my father felt a tremendous loss. The tears flowed freely from a man I had rarely seen crying.

At one particularly painful moment of emptiness he sobbed almost without control. He looked up at me with an expression of apology. "I guess everyone thinks I'm a big baby," he choked out. "No one thinks you're a big baby," I assured him. I reached out with love and touched his handsome face of wrinkles and tears.

In addition to the tears I also saw a sharpening of his wit. Not one to usually make many jokes, he was saying some very funny things in the days that followed my mother's death.

He was dressed for the funeral, and we were getting ready to leave for the church. He reached in his pants pocket and pulled out a handkerchief to once again wipe away the tears.

My fifteen-year-old stepson was watching with sympathy and concern. Daddy looked up at Christopher and tried to explain his display of sadness in a way that this teenager would understand.

"If you're in love, this is the way you're going to feel when you lose them. There's just no getting around it. If you're not, you'll be damn glad they're gone."

We all laughed.

After the funeral he put his arm around the minister, and this eighty-two year old man who had experienced the love of one woman for more than half a century said, "Well, Father Fred, you're going to bury me, too, but you're not going to marry me."

We all laughed.

It proved to me that laughter during periods of grief is a self-defense mechanism, a survival tool, a relief, a momentary reversal of emotions. Laughter during sad times is a much needed and welcome change, no matter how brief.

Weathering Life's Storms

Even in a severe and threatening storm love can survive,
if we cling together for support and reassurance,
believing in the blue skies and calm seas of tomorrow.
But if we try to stand alone, brave and foolish,
our love can be lost and so can we.

CHAPTER 7

SHARING

If we're not careful, relationships can easily be destroyed by a death in the family. Husbands and wives driven apart by the loss of a child they both loved dearly . . . siblings separated over the death of a parent.

It doesn't matter what the relationship is, it can be broken by grief, if our grief becomes saturated with guilt and resentment. If we feel that the other person doesn't share our deep sense of loss, that's when the resentment starts to build. If we feel they didn't love the person as much as we did, we think they don't understand what we are now going through. If blame and guilt enter into one's feelings, the relationship becomes all the more vulnerable.

In both my former husband's suicide and my son's, I felt, at the time, if I had not been seeing Jack, they might not have happened.

Especially after Jody's death, it was hard not to push Jack away, punishing him and me for the time we'd spent together when I could have been with my son.

By doing so, I was declaring Jody my number one priority, even though he was dead, and proving that I was thinking more about my son than my lover. Jody might have doubted my love when he was alive, but I would clarify it now and be faithful to his memory. It's that kind of irrational thinking and misdirected loyalty to the memory of someone that can easily come between survivors.

It gets even more complicated and difficult if you resent someone for something they did or did not do while the other person was alive. Once Jack insisted that he and I go out instead of staying home and playing monopoly with Jody. I suggested that it was good for Jody to have Jack spending time with him. Jack said, "but what about us?" I went out that night but resented it, and resented it much more looking back after Jody's death.

Fortunately Jack wouldn't let me push him away and made me face those feelings and talk them out. He made me understand that he too regretted not spending more time with my son. That he desperately wished he had been more like a father and friend to Jody. He made me realize that I wasn't the only one hurting and wishing some things had been done differently. I wasn't the only one trying to come to terms with this terrible loss and Jack made me see that.

He also made it clear that destroying our relationship wasn't going to help anyone, and it certainly wouldn't bring Jody back. With Jack's guidance we both survived and so did our relationship.

Jay and Marilyn Mossman also survived, but it was a desperate struggle to hold onto one another. A struggle that began in 1980 when their sixteen year old son, Jay, Jr., killed himself.

The agony of grief left Marilyn weak and lifeless. Jay went on almost in a normal state. He declared right away that this tragedy would not ruin their lives. He was determined not to let his son's irrational act pull the rest of the family down or drive them apart.

Marilyn already felt ruined, and wanted, at times, to desperately follow her child into death.

Jay went to work. Marilyn stayed home without the physical strength to prepare a meal or do a load of laundry. On weekends Jay worked on the lawn and in the flower gardens. Marilyn stayed in bed, depressed and weak.

Marilyn would sit at the dinner table and cry rather than eat. Jay would often look at her without understanding. One night, weeks after the suicide, Jay said, "What's the matter, did something happen?"

"Yes," Marilyn said with bitterness and resentment, "our son died."

Jay felt anger because he thought Marilyn should pull herself together and go on as before.

She felt resentment because he didn't understand why she couldn't.

At that point, they weren't talking to each other about what they were feeling. They were just feeling it and letting it come between them.

Several months after their son's death Jay insisted that they have the annual company employee party as they had done for the past several summers. Marilyn didn't want to, but she didn't tell Jay that. Instead, she decided to try to do what she thought was important to him.

She says it was horrible. Jay, who wasn't feeling well the day of the party, went to bed as soon as everyone left.

Marilyn, depressed and weak, having used all the energy she could muster to try and be a good hostess, was left to clean up the mess.

The resentment built. There was no real communication.

Marilyn says if Jay had left her when she was feeling that way she wouldn't have tried to stop him.

MARJORIE WHITE

She didn't leave him, she says, because she didn't have the energy to pack a suitcase. Jay thought if Marilyn would make herself do things, get out and see people as he was doing, that she'd snap out of her feelings of despair.

Fortunately, Marilyn was seeing a therapist who helped her work through these feelings, and the Mossmans started going to "The Compassionate Friends." "The Compassionate Friends" is a support group for people trying to cope with the death of a child. A little later they also started attending meetings of "Seasons," a support group for the survivors of suicide.

Jay realized that he hadn't allowed himself to grieve, and that he had been very uncomfortable with Marilyn's grief.

It took Marilyn two years of intense grieving before she felt she was on the way to recovery.

It took Jay almost two years to begin to grieve, to release the feelings he had been suppressing all those months.

It took the support of "The Compassionate Friends" and "Seasons," and their loving daughter, who says she was sure her parents were going to split, to re-cement this marriage.

They learned the importance of communication, and of reaching out to one another and to those around them.

They are now one of the most sharing couples I've ever met.

When Marilyn speaks, she looks at Jay for reassurance. When Jay talks of his pain, he holds Marilyn's hand for the comfort of her closeness. When his eyes become red and rimmed with tears she smiles a soft and gentle smile that tells him it's okay.

Marilyn and Jay Mossman now give a lot of their time and energy to help other people face, and cope with, their losses. They try to help people avoid what almost happened to them; what can so easily happen, and does, to many couples—the loss of each other after the loss of a child.

Support groups can have an important, sometimes life saving, place in surviving the ordeal of personal loss.

By sharing feelings and thoughts, strengths and weaknesses, the pits and pitfalls we can see that we aren't alone, and that we aren't crazy, or going crazy, because of what we are thinking, and the way we are feeling, physically, as well as emotionally. We can see that others have felt the same way and made it through that dark tunnel of desolation caused by such a tragic loss, and been able to emerge out into the light of acceptance where the wounds can heal, and we can discover that we really do want to live again.

Facing the Uncertain

When there is something big,
and uncertain to face,
a comforting, reassuring hand
can help us overcome the anxiety we feel,
allowing us to accomplish
what we could never do alone.

O'Donnell and Steve
"The christening of Brian and David"

"They have chosen to chance it"

CHAPTER 8

FACING THE FUTURE

It's hard to face the future without fear when tragic loss lives in your past.

In fact, it is impossible to be entirely free of the thought that you might feel such pain again.

It's hard to remarry after a devastating divorce.

It's hard to be carefree about the birth of a new baby if you've experienced the death of a child.

But to protect yourself completely from the possibility of pain is to shut yourself off from the probability of joy.

It's a fact of life—that to love deeply leaves you open for hurt.

My daughters, Marjorie and O'Donnell, lost a father and brother and can't help fearing that something terrible might happen to their husbands or children.

But they have chosen to chance it. They decided to love and to give life. They do it for the days of happiness, the months of joy, and for a future of feeling, rather than a cold and uncaring life protected from pain.

We cannot get the most out of life if we don't give freely of ourselves, including our emotions. I think to shut down those feelings after experiencing grief is a big mistake.

Marjorie and her husband Jody
"The christening of Jonathan"

I believe I love even more strongly and openly now because I know what it's like when a special outlet for that love is lost. And so I've loved without restraint my first grandchild, Emily, and the others who have followed. But there have been fears and tears.

When O'Donnell and her husband Steve found out that their second pregnancy was producing twins, I squealed and cried for joy. When the boys were born six weeks premature and one of them, little David, was in danger of dying, I cried for fear of never knowing him.

When he came home from the hospital several weeks after his brother Brian, I cried again with grateful thanks.

When Marjorie was going through the long and difficult labor of her first child, I cried for fear that something would happen to her, or that she would have to face another tragic loss. A caesarean section was performed, and a precious new life was saved. I cried with relief. And when I saw little Jonathan in her arms being held close to her breasts, I cried for the joy that she would now know.

And I smiled because I knew that joy would allow the pain and fear just experienced to be forgotten, both hers and mine.

There will be other pain and lots of fear, for all of us, but there will also be genuine joy because we have allowed ourselves to go on being vulnerable. We have chosen to live and love and give life everything we've got in order to get the most we can, for as long as we can.

The HEDGES
2859-63-65 BENSON

FIVE GENERATIONS

"Why is everyone so happy when I'm so sad?"

CHAPTER 9

SPECIAL DAYS

Birthdays, holidays, anniversaries, vacations, all the special times become the hard times during periods of grief, when the loss is new.

Even years later we can feel cheated because that special someone isn't there to share this special day.

It can also be a terrible time of resentment. You remember the day the divorce became final. You remember the day your child died, his birthday and what he wore at the beach that last summer he was alive, what he gave you on your birthday; why doesn't everyone else?

Christmas isn't the same without them there to cut the tree, and to guess what's in every gayly wrapped package, as they always did.

It seems no one notices their absence but you.

Why is everyone so happy when you're so sad? The truth is you're trying to make each special occasion seem the same. It is not the same, and can never be the same again.

You don't speak of the one who is missing, and neither does anyone else, for fear of upsetting you. You set the mood and the remembrance level. If you remember with ease, so will everyone else. If you don't say their name, neither will the others.

Each year I remember Jody's birthday and the day he committed suicide quietly to myself. So do my daughters. Each year I let it pass without a big deal or a mention, so do my daughters. But we're thinking about it. We haven't forgotten, none of us has. Why not share a little remembrance that would make everyone feel better? Something that would bring us together rather than isolate us from each other. It's too easy to start feeling like a martyr for not forgetting, to feel more loving and sensitive than someone who might have forgotten.

It's so easy to feel unloved, left out and alone, on special days, and make others feel guilty because we do. But just as with the rest of the year we need to share our feelings, our thoughts and needs so that others can understand and respond with comfort and sympathy and helpful diversions.

Nine years after Jody spent his last Christmas with us, and twelve years after her father died, Marjorie wrote this poem that touched me deeply and made me realize that none of us ever forgets. We remember in different ways. The important thing is that we do, and that we share it.

Christmas '85

The leaves have fallen.
We can see Mimi's white Christmas lights now,
instead of just the string.
The snow begins to fall,
and we wait for the phone to ring.
It's great-Grandma worrying if all
are snug at home.
The wood is in a pile,
under the maple.
For awhile it blocks the path
to Mimi's house.
The sheep hang out in the barnyard.
We wait for the lambs that everyone loves, until they grow up.
The snowsuits come out as we become children again,
waiting to share the excitement of
snow angels and sled rides with those still
too young to care.
We hope and pray that they will know that joy.
On the way to the pine forest to cut our Christmas tree,
we look over at the hill,
at the graves of those we love and miss.
And as their faces and voices flood our minds,
we pray that they are at peace.
We are glad that they are so near.
The inside trees are up.
We try once again to remember the story,
where did the tradition begin?
The presents begin to pile.
We sometimes forget the joy of giving;
thankfully not for long.
Yes, it's Christmas time again,
at "The Hedges."

Marjorie White Westerlund

(The "mimi" referred to in poem is me—That's what my grandchildren call me.)

This Christmas there is a new grave over on the hill. Great Grandma died in August and she now rests there, at peace, we pray. Her holiday presence will be missed. Christmas morning breakfast will not be the same. Though we will go over to Great Granddaddy's house, and fix omelets, and drink champagne, someone very special will be missing. We'll try to make do. We'll smile and pretend that we are happier than we really feel. But we will remember, and we will mention her name, and we'll find new joys, new ways of making the holidays happy times, and not times of ever-lasting, unforgivable, unmentionable loss.

MARJORIE WHITE

"We can help ourselves by helping others"

CHAPTER 10

COMFORT IN CARING

For many of us the healing process can be completed by reaching out to help others. We use what we have been through to help family and friends, as well as strangers, face, or in some cases, try to avoid, difficult times in their lives.

It is the reason I started speaking openly about suicide, when it was not an accepted or popular thing to do. It has helped me to know that, by being honest about the tragedies in my life, other families going through a similar situation won't feel as closed off from society as those dealing with suicide once did.

Allowing others to share what we have learned from personal adversity can bring about widespread understanding and change that can help us all. It is the reason I wrote "Everything To Live For." In that book I take a very hard look at my son's life and death in hopes of preventing other young people from taking their lives. With "Everything To Live For" I'm trying to help parents avoid the terrible pain of losing a child to suicide. There are heartfelt and comforting rewards in knowing that something you do can make a difference, and actually save young lives.

Doing what we can to help others, and in turn to help ourselves, can take many forms.

For some people I've met it's holding a backyard carnival for the Muscular Dystrophy Association.

One woman whose daughter died from cystic fibrosis started a community walk-a-thon to raise money for the association fighting that disease. Writer Frank De Ford, whose daughter also died from cystic fibrosis, used his talents and emotions and experience to write the book "Alex," which was turned into a t.v. movie. He wanted to help make people aware of this childhood killer in hopes something could be done to find a cure for C.F. and spare other parents the pain he and his wife went through. I'm sure his writing and sharing has helped him heal.

Marilyn and Jay Mossman now spend much of their time counseling and consoling, conducting seminars, and sharing in every way that they can what they have learned as a result of their son's suicide. They are active in two support groups, "The Compassionate Friends" (for families that have experienced the death of a child) and "Seasons" (for families and friends of a suicide victim).

They are the leaders of the local chapter of the "National Committee for Youth Suicide Prevention."

John Walsh, whose son, Adam, was abducted and murdered, has caused a whole nation to become sensitized to the problem of missing children.

For every possible personal challenge and conflict I can cite examples of individual courage that have inspired and helped us all.

The point is we can make a difference in each other's lives. We can repair our own life while helping to improve the existence of our neighbor.

The individual can be strong and powerful. I think sometimes we forget just how powerful.

It's important that we don't forget. It can actually mean the difference between life and death, ours and others.

The Strength of One

We must never underestimate
our own strength or importance.
One person can make a difference,
even when weakened by grief, despair and loneliness.
Adversity can sometimes cause our
roots to reach out for the waters of wisdom,
strengthening our heart and soul, and
enhancing our beauty of purpose.

Road of Life

How can we know where the road of life will lead?
How can we be sure what's down the unpredictable path of existence,
beyond the veils of light and darkness?
How can we see around the corner of uncertainty?
We can't.
Do we continue to venture into the unknown when the known has
hurt us terribly?
Do we keep going forward when our past is paved with pain?
We must.
We can't stop in our tracks and hurt forever.
We must allow the detours, wrong turns and back roads of our past
to serve as guideposts into the future . . .
and we do have a future.
We can't stop being mobile.
We can't stand still.
To stop is to give up on the promise of life;
the love, the laughter that might also be down the road.
Can we throw up our hands, rather than reach out for help?
We can't.
We can't because others have shown us that we can feel differently
than we do today.
We can heal. The tears can dry and the comfort of caring can once
again replace the emptiness inside.
The smiles can become real, the love sincere.

We can once again travel with confidence and reassurance,
if we discard the baggage of bitterness, self-pity, and self-destruction,
if we travel on with only love for ourselves and others,
and not dwell on the pain in our past
or worry about what adversity might lay ahead.
The road of life may be very rough at times
but if we don't travel it at all,
we chance missing some breathtaking scenery,
some moving moments . . .
people and places, sentiments and times to be remembered.
Sometimes beyond the roughest road,
or the most perplexing crossroad,
lays the smooth surface of understanding.
We must not stop or turn back when there is a breakdown,
a misfortune, or no clear route.
Sometimes we must travel blindly
until our direction becomes clear to us and others.
There are many weary travelers on the road of life.
Many temporarily lost in the grief of passing.
The road to recovery is never easy.
But it can lead to insight, understanding and love.

SUSAN WHITE-BOWDEN

MARJORIE WHITE

"It's ok to look to the future"

CHAPTER 11

GOING ON WITH HOPE

As I said in the introduction, there is no precise formula for coping with personal loss. However, the ingredients of acceptance, forgiveness, faith and the other survival tools I've talked about, should always be there in varying degrees. Some people need more of one ingredient than another. Some rely very heavily on their faith in God to help them through.

Some rely strongly on sharing with a special friend or group. Whatever combination works for you is the right one, but a blend of all these ingredients is needed for balance and stability.

Some people try to put the subject of the loss very distantly in the past. They never visit the grave or even try to keep the memory of the deceased close. They try to let go completely. I personally don't think that's the way to healthy healing. I've never tried to do that, I couldn't, even if I wanted to. My life has been irreversibly changed by each death, because each life, I believe has had such a profound effect on what I was and who I am now.

People have asked me why I still haven't let go of Jody almost ten years after his death?

The simple answer is I don't want to. I still feel the warmth of love when I think of him. I still laugh when I think of some of the witty and wacky things he said and did. I still cry when the loneliness of his absence pierces my heart. I can be driving on a familiar road that we traveled together, or hear a certain song on the car radio, and I miss him as much as if he died yesterday.

It doesn't happen that often anymore, but I think it always will, from time to time, as long as I live and choose to allow Jody to go on living in my heart and mind.

It is only because I have chosen to keep the memory of Jody's life and death so fresh within me that I have been able to write about him, and lecture to teenagers and parents about teen suicide.

It's why I have been able to work so hard to keep other kids from following in his footsteps, and hopefully keep other parents from feeling the pain of such a tragic loss.

However, I have started cutting back on the number of speaking engagements I'm doing. I have started saying no, and I'm working very hard not to feel guilty when I do that.

The truth is that each time I speak on the subject I am reopening the wound. I just can't share my story without bleeding emotionally, and I'm just not letting myself heal completely. So I've made the decision to back off a bit, to give myself a little more healing time without stopping my work completely. I do know, from the response of those I've talked to and the hundreds of letters I've gotten, that lives can be saved by telling my story, so I just can't stop altogether. But I think all of us who choose to open up our lives in an effort to help others must be careful that our cause doesn't completely take over our existence, to the detriment of our families and our other responsibilities. Some people can lead a crusade or start a foundation without the daily reminder of their pain destroying their mental or physical health. For some, it gives them reason and purpose just when they need it most. It becomes worthwhile work serving the needs of many while satisfying a deep need of those performing the service. Humanitarian acts can help the healing process in a miraculous way.

But don't be ashamed to think about yourself and what you want and to move on when you're ready.

In fact, at times you need to be selfish.

That can mean new loves and when you're ready a new life and a new direction.

With healing comes a promise that it's okay to look to the future without forgetting the past. Necessarily, each loss causes changes, and we can't help but be influenced by it. The bigger the loss, the bigger the change. We will never be the same again. But we can go on, eventually with new energy and new direction. With healing comes the happiness of hope, the strength of survival, the understanding of self, the freedom of choice, the ability to laugh and to cry, and the opportunity to live on with a heart that has healed.

MARJORIE WHITE

MARJORIE WHITE

The Garden of Hope

There are many colors in the Garden of Hope.

The green of youth,
bright and full of promise,
grown old, it's dark and dignified.

The red is love, life's necessary blood,
sometimes passionate and painful,
but without it there are no family or friends.

The soft pink provides the warmth of flesh,
a tenderness that cries for closeness.
The peace of a baby just bathed and fed.

The blue is misty emotion,
like lakes and rain and gentle tears.
A refuge, an outlet, on a dismal day.

The yellow is the essence of hope,
sunshine and happiness,
the color of light and loveliness.

Yellow is the soft hue of caring and companionship,
reflected in daisies and daffodils,
touching the sensitive and soulful.

In the summertime this garden is glorious,
but in the fall of discontent it fades.
In the winter of despair it dies.

Patience and seasons bring change.
The frozen sod of sadness softens,
renewed life buds and bursts into bloom.

These flowers seem more vivid and valuable.
This garden is cherished so much more,
because in our grief we lived without it.

The return of hope,
is the return of life,
the greens, the reds and the yellows.

From my garden of hope
Comes the joy of all joys
Children and grandchildren
The promise that there will be a future